ENGLISH QABALLA

THE MYSTERY OF THE LETTERS

ISBN 978-1-915933-20-1 (Hardcover)
ISBN 978-1-915933-21-8 (Paperback)

A catalogue for this title is available from the British Library.
10 9 8 7 6 5 4 3 2 1

First published in 2024 by Hadean Press
West Yorkshire
England

WWW.HADEANPRESS.COM

ENGLISH QABALLA

THE MYSTERY OF THE LETTERS

Cath Thompson

For Jim

CONTENTS

A fool takes in all the lumber of every sort that he comes across, so that the knowledge which might be useful to him gets crowded out, or at best is jumbled up with a lot of other things, so that he has a difficulty in laying his hands upon it. Now the skilful workman is very careful indeed as to what he takes into his brain-attic. He will have nothing but the tools which may help him in doing his work, but of these he has a large assortment, and all in the most perfect order.

A Study in Scarlet, by Sir Arthur Conan Doyle

Prologue

Several different schools of thought have pointed at the present era as a time of great change. The advent of the English Qaballa is symptomatic of that noticeable shift. In the hundred years since the writing of the *Book of the Law*[1] every area of human endeavour has been reformed with new science, new technology, new materials, and new ideas. Magic is not exempted from this, since its practitioners are necessarily of their own time and social environment, with mental processes and vocabularies adapted for the contemporary modern world. The unforeseeable new factor in magic is a proof of mathematical design in the English language called English Qaballa, an evolutionary step forward out of the near paralysis that resulted from the Magickal Revival of Crowley's generation.

This is my seventh book about English Qaballa. I have done what I set out to do after James Lees died, namely, to put into the public domain a record

---

1 Publisher's note: *The Book of the Law*, otherwise known as *Liber AL vel Legis* or *Liber AL* (originally *Liber L*), was dictated to Aleister Crowley in Cairo in 1904 with the assistance of his wife and Scarlet Women, Rose Edith Kelly. Numerous editions of this text have been published and it can now easily be found online.

of the work that he did with EQ and show that what he discovered is a complete system of initiatory magical theory and practice. Jim wanted recognition for his magical work but had no desire for fame or followers. We had composed an EQ guidebook and a number of other essays over the years, and we agreed that I would write for publication one day. I chose to write a set of books rather than attempt one big tome because I thought I had a better chance of completing my task in separate stages. My first notion was a set of four volumes and Hadean Press came up with a very pleasing cover design that was adaptable to the colour theme of the four Elements; this plan was too well laid, however, and all went agley after the third book was published.

My first book, dealing with various techniques and methods of English Qaballa, was a challenge which I met with enthusiasm. We had compiled a decent first draft which needed some additional material and editing, and I made a good job of it. The second book was put together from our notes and pre-existing unpublished articles about astrologically timed rituals, with personal records detailing their performance and effect, and this too presented no great difficulties. Pleased with my literary efforts thus far, I went on to write a history of EQ. This was also partly autobiographical as I had encountered the new gematria and joined the group of pioneering first generation E. Qaballists just four years after Jim had obtained the magical alphabet. I enjoyed writing this book. My account stops just short of our great ritual experiment of 2010, and I meant to go on to a full description of this work in the next volume.

However, I had determined to move, and my career as an author went on hold while I attended to the business of buying and selling property. Not knowing how long this would take and not wishing to retire my magical work, I devised a project to seek out spirits à la grimoire in the *Book of the Law*. I found that they were there, and that I had the makings of a Tarot deck based on EQ. This became the subject of the fourth book, by demand, though I omitted the spirit workings on the grounds that they were perhaps too subjective to be of any practical value to anyone else. The Tarot was inspired from start to finish and later I considered that it had been the speaking of my Magical Word as a magician, but at the time the book was a nuisance. It bulged and split into two and then had to be stitched back together again but I had run out of steam and some of the material was awkwardly presented.

My fifth book details perhaps our most important contribution to modern occultism, an initiatory formula linked directly to the Zodiac, the Moon and the Sun. The efficacy of the 418 rituals has been independently proven by several individuals. The challenge I faced with writing the fifth book was to stay within the bounds of my Magical Oath while presenting enough information for the brave adventurer to embark upon the astrological journey. This I did. The next work was one I had tried at least three times before, a fully enumerated *Book of the Law*, involving only graphic design and a lot of calculations.

The present work deals with the metaphysical paradigm that is revealed by the application of English Qaballa to the *Book of the Law*. To avoid unnecessary repetition, I have assumed some foreknowledge of EQ and its source text on the part of the reader. I have described the mystical philosophy of EQ approximately in the chronological order in which it evolved out of the research and experimentation carried out by the first generation of E. Qaballists. The non-denominational spirituality at the core of EQ is a platform from which to negotiate a secure magical reality amidst the hurly-burly and incessant monkey-chatter of the present era. It upholds a coherent star-based system that emphasises the Goddess and the female principle and provides the foundation of a magical synthesis for self-initiation.

The method of Science is to ask questions, of which there will always be more, and the aim of Religion is to provide answers, of which there will always be doubt. I have compared notes with Hebrew scholars and Freemasons and Buddhists and alchemists and shamans, to the shared enjoyment and surprise revelations of all concerned. The English Qaballa, along with its particular relevance to women's occult work, is a metaphysical discovery that combines scientific approach and religious aspiration in a psycho-cosmological model that functions admirably in its own terms and coherently in parallel with other systems of magic.

Thanks to Barry Down BA Hons (Bro. Hersechel) for much encouragement and indulgence during the writing of this book.

Cath Thompson 2023
ESTE LEX DARE

THE *BOOK OF THE LAW*

The *Book of the Law* was received in the watershed period marking the end of the Victorian Age and the beginning of the Atomic Age, in the first decade of the 20th century. The writing in April 1904 took place within a few years of such events as the Wright brothers making their first successful flight and the first production of the Ford Model T motor car; after Max Planck had formulated his quantum theory but before Einstein had created his special theory of relativity, between the birth of Walt Disney and the death of Mark Twain.

The end of the 19th century was the adulthood of the first generation born under the presence of Neptune, the planet discovered in 1846. There was an upsurge of interest in matters traditionally ruled by the Twelfth Zodiac House and Sign of the Fishes, Pisces, the natural domain of the mystical Neptune. Magical effects were being produced by new technology as well as by illusionists. The novelists of the period were creating science and detective fiction, featuring original dramatic characters armed for good or ill with mysterious and secret knowledge. Innovative and unreliable new medicines and health cures flourished; and there was a proliferation of secret organisations, religious movements, and magical societies.

In this period of spiritual and metaphysical renaissance and revolutionary zeal for exploring intangible ideas and unseen forces beyond the visible spectrum the expansion of human knowledge was getting ahead of its religious inheritance. Even as the increased speed of communications and ease of transport had encouraged a cautious mingling of esoteric traditions from around the globe, the Biblical foundation of the Industrial Revolution was being deconstructed by scientific reason as social evolution clashed with ancient taboo.

In 1904 the age of steam was giving way to the age of electricity. Radio broadcasting was being invented, work was starting on the Panama Canal, and the Cubist art movement was just beginning. Publications in that year included Sigmund Freud's *The Psychopathology of Everyday Life* and Marie Curie's *Recherches sur les substances Radioactive*. New sciences were asking new questions, these answers were about to transform the whole world, placing increasing pressure upon religious establishments to reassure the faithful, and maintain authority according to pre-industrialised custom. New spiritual and philosophical ideas were world-wide. The Theosophical movement had become one of the most popular alternative religions in the U.S.A.; the Hermetic Order of the Golden Dawn, founded in London four years after Blavatsky's death, was one of the most productive magical organisations in Europe; in Germany the O.T.O. was just achieving recognition. This was the fertile soil into which the seed called *Liber Al* was dropped.

Crowley, who was already an accomplished poet, traveller, and mountaineer, had become a member of the Golden Dawn six years before the events in Cairo occurred. Rather in the manner of a Greek tragedy, he was chosen to be the scribe for a message which he could never decode, and although he fully grasped its significance, he was unable to prove it. Without the key to the 'war-engine' Crowley could not himself start it even if he did glimpse what it might accomplish. In consequence his extraordinary attempt to formulate a unified occult philosophy lacked the vital ingredient of a new aeon, namely, new interpretation and understanding of pre-existing conditions. In any case, the Old Aeon was about to explode into the mayhem and slaughter of two World Wars, by the end of which there was another new planet to be reckoned with, and a new era had undeniably begun. The dawn of the New Aeon and the writing of the *Book of the Law* was also the ending of the Age of Abraham, whose last prophet was indeed Mohammed, peace be unto him.

THE PROOF OF THE *BOOK OF THE LAW*

The proof of the *Book of the Law* is the fact that it contains its own gematria. The text, which refers to an 'order & value of the English Alphabet' and the finding of 'new symbols to attribute,' was dictated to Crowley almost exclusively in the English language. The full alphabet had not then had four centuries of use, the consonant J only becoming differentiated from the vowel I in English books from the mid-17th century: yet, unaccountably, the English system of gematria works. That is to say, the numeric values generated by the revised alphabetical sequence and applied to the text in the usual way provide connections between particular words, showing them to express meanings which are in parallel, alike or contrariwise, as if on the same frequency or resonating from the same source; these connections are quantifiable, allowing scientific analysis to interpret the text in its own context and not only with reference to the text but to the whole reality that the language is capable of encompassing.

The English Qaballistic Alphabet is as follows: A=1, L=2, W=3, H=4, S=5, D=6, O=7, Z=8, K=9, V=10, G=11, R=12, C=13, N=14, Y=15, J=16, U=17, F=18, Q=19, B=20, M=21, X=22, I=23, T=24, E=25, P=26.

It is unaccountable, for English vocabulary is an orderly confusion of incorporated spellings and meanings, translated from various sources in different historical periods and added to the native language in the course of its development; but how all was made to fulfil the requirements of a system of numeric correspondences it is impossible to declare. More improbable still are the numerically correspondent words that did not exist in 1904, appearing in the language by future literary invention or by translation from historical documents not yet discovered.

The proving of the new Holy Book is precisely this demonstration of numeric structure embedded in language. Phonetic symbols obeying mathematical laws are suggestive of deliberate design and moreover, are supportive of Crowley's claim regarding the dictation of the manuscript – he could not have composed that text. The enumeration could not be a man-made phenomenon, it is too coherent for that. English Qaballa is by its very existence strong evidence in favour of Crowley's assessment, indicative of mathematical design embedded in the English language with a cipher key hidden by the Scribe's own unwitting hand in the manuscript of *Liber Al*. The evidence is in favour of Something having deliberately overseen the development of the English language, and of all its component languages. A mysterious Something so skilled in numerology that it is not bound by number nor contained by mathematical laws, something in accordance with the nature of which the numbers themselves exist. The evidence puts *Liber Al* into the catalogue of miraculous weirdness that afflicts the reasoning mind and reinforces the faithful heart.

THE ENGLISH QABALLISTIC KEY TO *LIBER AL*

The English Qaballistic Key to *Liber Al* was obtained in 1976 by an English magician named James Lees. He was an experienced astrologer and Kabbalist who was leading a knowledgeable group of ceremonial occultists in the English Midlands. They were the first English Qaballists. Back in the early days of English Qaballa the obvious thing to do with it was to apply it to the *Book of the Law*, the text from which it was obtained. Later on, of course, study of the new gematria became more diverse, but for the first explorers the *Book of the Law*, the source of EQ, was the mystery to be investigated. They agreed that the text could not have been invented by human hand to contain the system of correspondences that had been revealed in 1976. The assignment of numeric values to the twenty-six letters of the English Alphabet created linkages between words derived from ancient cultures and from modern paradigms, all within the limits of the Book's own vocabulary. From this arose a credible idea of a deliberate pattern in the Universe, and an inclination to view the Book with some respect. The pioneers explored the new correspondences and making notes, they began the custom of capitalising words to accentuate the symbolic virtue rather than the literal meaning.

They studied and meditated and talked and started to devise the first ritual experiments with which to prove the system.

Having established prima facie evidence of *Liber Al*'s credibility as a Holy Book, the initial study of the gematria spread slowly from the text. The enumeration of the English Alphabet soon provided a variety of simple letter correspondences to indicate that the correct order and value had been obtained. For instance, the letter M has the value 21 which is 3x7. The number 7 traditionally belongs to the Goddess, and this shows the feminine nature of the initial M, while 7 is the value of O, another essentially female symbol. The English spelling of the great syllable OM therefore adds to 28 which is the value of WORD and HOLY, a pretty little correspondence. The letter G, significant in Freemasonry, retains its mystery as the 11th letter of the E. Qaballistic alphabet, 11 being the key to the cipher; and the suggestion of the two Pillars in the repeated digits occurs again in the value of the word ELEVEN=101. The letter T is the same shape as the upper-case Greek Tau, the early Christian symbol of conversion; in EQ the emphasis is an unqualified deity, for T=24=GOD. The lunar number 13 is the value of the crescent-shaped letter C. The half-circle of the letter D with its value

6=LAW indicates the mathematical basis of the system. And the central mystery is in the letter A=1, where ONE=WOMAN, because this Holy Book with its built-in gematria is part of the New Aeon and the renaissance of the Goddess.

These correspondences demonstrate the workings of English gematria, grouping words with particular meaning and significance according to numeric value, and discovering their connectivity.

The Feminine Principle

The feminine principle is emphasised throughout the *Book of the Law*; even THE LAW has the same value as YONI, 59. The Supreme Goddess is characterised as Nuit, 'Queen of Infinite Space and the Infinite Stars thereof'. Her arched body is the 'gemmed azure' of the starry sky as portrayed on the Stele of Revealing and in the pharaonic chambers of Ancient Egypt. NUIT=78, the numerical symbol of Infinite Space, where 7=O and 8 is Infinity; the O as both the letter and the symbol of Zero represents the emptiness of Space, or Nothing. The Element of FIRE=78 belongs to Her, as does the South Cardinal Zodiac Sign CANCER=78, the astrological ruler of the Mother, the home and the hearth. The spiritual Fire of Creation, the womb of Space, the nurturing of the human animal, all are concordant with the number 78, Zero expressed to Infinity.

Nuit is not spoken of 'as one, but as none'. The philosophy of EQ proposes a dimension of Nothingness outside Time/Space. This is a Nothingness about which almost nothing can be said, for it is without quality or quantity or characteristics of any knowable sort. It is None of anything, an inconceivable Perfection symbolised by 0 with no beginning nor end, a pure continuity. In the manifest Universe it is represented by the infinite reach of space. Its most recognisable qualities are of containing and being Not, so that chaos and disorder are as non-existent as harmony and rhythm. These concepts arrive later on in the story, after the balance of perfection has been interrupted.

In this context *Liber Al* says 'the Perfect and the Perfect are one Perfect – nay, are None!' and 'Had! The manifestation of Nuit,' where HAD=11. This double-digit number is a key to understanding the unknown omnipresent Nothing symbolised by Nuit, Queen of Infinite Space, for it is that Nothing that divides for love's sake. The One (1) is None and so Eleven (11) symbolises the double negative of divided Nothing.

Nuit is infinite nothingness, from which Creation occurs by means of the division for love's sake, and the 'chance of union' which forms a positive state out of the divided negative. Naught can come from the division of Nothing except Less-than-Nothing, and it is the union of these two negative states that creates the positive. The matriarchal signature on the work of Creation is plainly seen through the E. Qaballistic lens.

A DISTURBANCE IN THE PERFECTION

The disturbance in the perfection of Nothing is Hadit, the infinitely tiny particle in the infinitely large space. HADIT=58=LIBRA the Sign of the Scales. Hadit is the potential energy at the fulcrum, the almost invisible movement that must tip the balance into manifesting the potential matter of Nuit. 58 symbolises Energy (5) expressed to Infinity (8). 58 is the value of ZODIAC, indicating that all twelve signs partake of this primordial force of disturbance in nothingness. Astrological correspondences in the text of *Liber Al* are significant since astrology has accompanied humanity's spiritual evolution throughout history. Celestial observations are a foundation of magical and religious practice worldwide, and English Qaballa is no exception.

The transformation of Nothing is the death of its perfection. Following the disturbed balance of Hadit/Libra is Scorpio, the sign of Death. LIBRA+SCORPIO=151=CERTAINTY, the tangible effect of these two signs is beyond doubt as all physical life is eventually judged unfit for purpose and discontinued. Scorpio is like a reset button in the progress of the Zodiac, bringing the predictable course of events to a halt. Astrological divinations are equivocal when the Moon is in Scorpio, as the paradoxical condition that the luminary mediates from there is certain to cause events to die or alter irrevocably in the most unexpected way, which is nearly always unfortunate. SCORPIO=93=DIVIDE and also UNITY. In English Qaballa 93 signifies the necessity of the impossible. In the Solar year it is the middle of Autumn, with festivals and remembrances for the dead. In the lunar cycle, which correlates with human fertility, it is the menstrual period.

BLOOD=42=STAR

Menstrual blood is the most magically significant human bodily secretion. Blood is the vehicle of life, maintaining organic health and distributing the physical elements of nourishment within the body. Loss of this precious fluid can be risky, even catastrophic, which is why red is the colour used for a danger signal. The exception is menstrual blood which cleanses and prepares the womb for a new incarnation, a contrarily safe haemorrhage consistent with the unpredictability of Moon in Scorpio.

BLOOD=42=STAR

confirming the relationship between humanity and the Cosmos, and the separate individuality indicated by *Liber Al* in 'every man and every woman is a star.' This correspondence was immediately suggestive of the relevance of astrological tradition, which is perhaps the oldest system of living correspondences known to mankind, to the elucidation of *Liber Al* by English Qaballa.

42=CROSS indicates the sacrificial nature of the energy exchange from Spirit to the four Elements, a sacrifice that is reflected again in the menstrual flow. The connection with the symbolism of the Crucifixion is upheld at Easter, the Christian festival happening at the first full Moon after the Spring Equinox and therefore always a Moon in Libra/Scorpio festival. The menstrual flow is woman's blood sacrifice, 'the best blood' according to *Liber Al*. Scorpio is the ENDING=93 when events BEGIN=93.

93 is the separation that joins, as the tree trunk divides the branches from the roots. 93=TIME, the medium of manifestation. Time is used for measuring distances between points in space. The Egyptian god TAHUTI=93 is most appropriately concerned with the calculation of measurements and is associated with the Moon. The Moon is intimately involved with the ever-changing rhythms of life on Earth, influencing the ebb and flow of the waters, moving through the Zodiac in calibration of the menstrual cycle, and reflecting the stellar powers into human existence on a regular basis. The connection of 93=LISTEN with the Moon is further emphasised in SOUND=49=MOON and the tradition that Tahuti/Thoth holds the secrets of correct pronunciation of magical words, God-Names and so on. SILENT=93 indicates the significance of Silence, such an obvious necessity for effective communication and reception that it needs no elaboration here; but it is worth noting that SILENCE=MAGICIAN. The vibrations of matter in space/time that constitute the frequency waves of sound are immediate to the Creation.

93=NATURE, the overriding force in the Universe, the MOTHER=93 of all who remains a VIRGIN=93. This paradox is NATURAL=VENUS and ensures the evolution of ORIGINAL=93 phenomena. From these correlations it follows that SCORPIO=93 is a magically potent Zodiac sign, and transits of the luminaries' mark interval periods in which the creative dynamic is accessible.

The Moon is a Key

MOON=49, the sum of 7x7. The number 7 is always associated with the Goddess, with Venus and with Babalon in particular, as the Moon is always associated with femininity. 49=MONAD. The word *monad* means a single unit, an element that subdivides in order to reunite for the purpose of reproduction, consonant with the division for love's sake. ALONE shares the same value, 49, encapsulating the lunar singularity.

The Moon is of course the nearest celestial body to the Earth, coiling round the orbital path of the planet as they move together through space. The progress of Life on Earth is as dependent upon the Moon as upon the Sun. The Moon reflects the changing astrological configurations as they occur, transmitting them into the realms of human consciousness. The Moon is a KEY=49 that opens each Zodiac sign in turn and transmits its particular influences for about two and a half days, providing regular opportunities for magical operations of every kind. Astrological synchronicity is one of the principles upon which the E. Qaballistic system is based: the Tropical Zodiac is preferred to the Sidereal for its correspondence with the agricultural seasons.

CROWN=49 is an interesting attribution. This item of regalia encircles the top of the head as if birthing the rest of the royal body upwards into a non-physical realm. The wearer is inevitably isolated by the symbolic reality of coronation, as the new-born is separated from the womb by the crowning moment and physical reality of birth. Thereafter events become more or less subject to change under the inconstant moon, reliably uncertain as She is. The traditional correspondence between female sexuality and the Moon is confirmed and expanded by EQ. The names MARY and ROSE add to 49, a correspondence of such significance as to require an exposition too great for the current work, but nonetheless worthy of note.

These correspondences account for the contrariness of women and the inexplicable shared knowledge they possess without knowing exactly what it is. Additionally, these correspondences make it clear that a woman is no more open to the evils of temptation than is a man, but it is her nature ($=93$) to serve evolution and to provoke change. They also explain the affinity with the Moon that magically inclined women share, which is more spiritual than physical, the Moon being the Mother of Magic.

The Ordeal X

LIBRA+SCORPIO=CERTAINTY

as execution follows judgement. The next Zodiac sign is Sagittarius, which has the same value as HEREAFTER. The alchemy of the Centaur rectifies the spiritual substance of the sacrifice, and the transformation is completed by CAPRICORN=121, Rex Mundi in the Zodiac and Baphomet as the embodying symbol of the Elemental forces in equilibrium. These four signs add to 418 by English Qaballa. The practical application of these Astro-qaballistic studies led to the construction of astrologically synchronised rituals designed to adjust personal consciousness and bring the operator into harmony with the cosmos.

The series of 418 rituals involve the operator in the physical realities of Death and Regeneration as played out in the seasons of the year and the female reproductive cycle, making preparations in consciousness for the relocation of the living spirit and relieving the fear of annihilation. Another ritual marking the conjunction of the Sun and Venus provokes a sequence of initiatory experiences in accord with the four stages of 418, known collectively as the Ordeal X. The 'five pointed star,' the shape specifically mentioned in

Liber Al, is continuously being drawn in space by these conjunctions. The Sun-Venus ritual involves the operator in the physical geometric reality of the alchemical wedding, resolving the conflicts of Reasoning Mind with Emotional Mind and stabilising the psyche. SUN+VENUS=107, KNOW+DARE+WILL=107, and SILENCE=107, gematria clearly indicating the importance of this stellar configuration for the MAGICIAN=107.

The Ordeal X is a transition, a crossing from one conscious state to another. The numeric value of THE ORDEAL X is 128 where 28=WORD and 1 is the numeric symbol of the Divine WOMAN=ONE. 128 is the value of SCARLET WOMAN where SCARLET=BALANCED=82, and 82 is the reward of 28. The Scarlet Woman is given all power, according to *Liber Al*; with the Elements of the psyche balanced in the manifest personality and contact established with the consciousness of universal Love, she is the embodiment of her magical Word. A woman is made in the image of the Goddess as a man is made in the image of the God, her magical personality consciousness framed in her female body has a negative polarity and instead of relinquishing control of a positive centre of male self-identity as happens to a man engaged in the magical journey, she accepts the responsibility of a central receptive female negativity. Magical polarity is a simple primitive factor determined by physiology, dictating no more than a subtle difference of approach. WOMAN=46 is the VOID=46 in which creation occurs.

THE COMPLETE TREE OF LIFE

NOTHING=97=PISCES, the twelfth sign of the Zodiac. In the LIFE=CYCLE of the Zodiac Pisces/Nothing gives birth to the BABE=ARIES, the first Zodiacal sign. The watery environment of the Fish is symbolic of the waters in which the foetus develops, and the breaking of the waters that accompany the beginning of the birthing labour. PISCES=NOTHING represents Life before birth or Manifestation.

97 is the value of RA HOOR KHUT, and the reward of HEAVEN=79. This is the gematria of 'Abrahadabra! The reward of Ra Hoor Khut,' in *Liber Al*. Analysis of the word Abrahadabra reveals ABRA=TWO, HAD=11, ABRA=TWO. These numbers correspond with 21=M 12=R, the letters at the centre of the E. Qaballistic exposition of AL II:76 known as the Complete Tree of Life. This holds the pattern of the traditional Kabbalistic Tree to be as the roots of MANIFESTATION=200, the sum of '24 89 R P S T O V A L,' and the Perfected Tree with Malkuth raised to Da'ath as the branches of Unmanifestation where LIBRA=58 is the sum of '4 63 8 A B K 2 4 A.' The trunk that unites and divides the two states is SCORPIO=93, the sum of 'L G M O R 3 Y X.' 93 is also the value of MERKABAH, the vehicle of mystical ascent in the Hebrew system.

The central O separates the M=21 and 12=R, illustrating the formula 0=2 hidden in the word Abrahadabra. The Perfected Tree corresponds with Heaven, from which Earth is separated by TIME=93. The advent of NATURE=93 is concordant with the Unmanifest balance of Libra/Hadit losing equilibrium in the moment of Creation. The structure of Manifestation achieves Perfection when Malkuth is raised to Da'ath. This is why perfect conditions are impermanent.

Any number may be applied to the Complete Tree of Life in order to examine different layers of gematria in the expressions of the number, from the most dense and material symbolism of Malkuth in manifestation to the most diffuse and spiritual symbolism that the mind is able to consider. The number 93, confirmed as one of the most significant numeric symbols in the English Qaballa, shows the Unmanifest Kether and Yesod to be 4+93=97=NOTHING, and Unmanifest Tiphareth is B=20+93=113=SPIRIT, when viewed through the lens of TIME=93. It is worth noting that MESSAGE=93 and MEDIUM=113.

NOTHING

NOTHING=97 is represented in the Cosmos as PISCES=97, the most ethereal of the Water signs. Imagination, dream, vision, illusion, madness, fantasy, and occultism, all are ruled by Pisces/ Nothing. The magician must learn to navigate this unstable environment of consciousness. The mind-mirror of Pisces shares the inconstancy of the Moon; the symbol of the Fish with its deathly associations connects with Scorpio. Pisces is traditionally ruled by JUPITER=143=PERFECT, and TERRIBLE; modern astrology has appointed NEPTUNE=INVISIBLE as co-ruler, and it is worth noting the explorations and developments of human consciousness that followed the discovery of Neptune in the mid-nineteenth century.

The three Water signs, Pisces, Scorpio, Cancer, are characteristically feminine, secretive, and emotionally intuitive. Cancer is the Cardinal sign, the dynamic first expression of the Watery Element in the Zodiac; in the astrological chart this is the midnight position from whence all starts to rise towards the new day. Scorpio is the Fixed Water sign of the 8th House leaning inexorably westwards, and Pisces the Mutable sign is the last to rise above the predawn east. The time before dawn is known to be a sensitive period when humans are particularly vulnerable as the 12th House is associated with isolation and sickness of the mind and body. It is worth noting that the 12th House rules detective work, an activity which requires a specific set of correspondences for success in observing and linking clues that must lead to the truth. That requirement applies to criminal and medical investigations as well as to magical work. Occultism and clairvoyance belong to Pisces, and the importance of clear-sighted and honest thinking cannot be overstated, for self-deception and madness are also 12th House matters.

CONSCIOUSNESS

In the English Qaballa CONSCIOUSNESS=153 is an infinitely large SPHERE=97 whereof the CENTRE=113=BELIEF/SPIRIT is 'I am'. Its energy is refined to undetectable levels of saturation. Its frequency wave is smaller than the smallest particle that can be used by science to detect its presence. It is the medium in which all the other waves of energy are propagated. This energy field manifesting in THE BIG BANG=153=CONSCIOUSNESS coalesces into the particles that are the basis of light and physical matter in space/time. 153=THE LOVE OF NU where NU=SOUL is the waveform hiding the smallest particle, Hadit. I BELIEVE=CONSCIOUSNESS indicating the continuous nature of Creation according to English Qaballa, forming the substance of the astral plane, of dream and imagination and thought and all the consciousness of material existence.

It is interesting that the basic curse ingredients of BELL, BOOK, and CANDLE add up to CONSCIOUSNESS.

The personal pronoun I has the value 23 which is half the value of ME=46. The self-awareness of "Me" is conceived and projected as the identifying "I" yet only a portion of self is represented. The impulse of energy given to the self's idea of "I" by others is described in EQ as YOU=39=MARS which is the planetary ruler of all energy. Mars is the ruler of SCORPIO=93 and 39 is the reward of 93, the value of THYSELF and BEING. This flow and return of energy to the self-aware identity can be accepted or dismissed once independence is gained. Human babies are certainly able to distinguish between different sounds before learning words with which to articulate thoughts. The personalised concept of "I" is at least in part fostered by expressions beginning with "You are" and the energy contained in the spoken word YOU=MARS, qualified with nouns and adjectives. Other people provide a lot of input for the individual to use or discard in self-definition. Information received in undiscriminating childhood ignorance tends to be rather formative, and it is usually unwise to attempt to undermine the foundations of the psyche. Acknowledgement followed by a credible alternative, satisfactory to both Reason and Emotion, is a safer move. The point at issue is the separation of the One into the Many and the desirability of redeeming that divided state, and how EQ presents the solution to this everlasting problem. The division for love's sake is inherent in the human experience of life, separated from the birth mother, physically isolated from the rest of nature and divided from the universal source of consciousness. Only love can unite the divided, as *Liber Al* says with the wisdom of the ages, Love is the Law.

The mind as the unit of consciousness identifies itself-awareness with the words I AM=45. The word NOT=45 is a complementary opposite of I AM, like the other side of the coin, an inevitable conjoined duality. The idea of that which "I am" is measured and defined according to that which "I am Not". The symbol 45 is thus a consequence of manifested Consciousness, encapsulating the reflection of the division for love's sake. I AM counted well has the same value as LIFE. Life is the essence of the statement "I am." Of course, I AM THAT I AM = 143 = PERFECT.

45=I AM/NOT delineates the disturbance of perfection in terms of human experience, demonstrating the problem of fixing a self-identity in an ever-changing environment. 45=HORUS is the force that resists the immobile; 45=JUDAS whose action is the betrayal of divine love; these are refractions of the division for love's sake, necessary for the manifestation and evolution of the human spirit. A definition of self may in time lose relevance to everything except preservation of self; it may be overthrown or undermined by changes beyond the control of self; and since magic operates by and large in the realm beyond the reasoning consciousness of self-identity it is well to learn flexibility of mind so as to be able to contemplate two opposing ideas at once and survive the destruction of both. Individual human consciousness is both divided and united with its limitless source, which extends beyond Time.

I THINK=NOTHING and counted well the total is 189=MY CONSCIOUSNESS, meaning that the essence of "I think" is in fact "my consciousness". I FEEL=93=BEING, and BE=45=NOT/I AM. The emotional weight given to particular thoughts may be divisive or integrating in its effect.

I AM = NOT is a difficult situation to negotiate, usually involving a breakdown of some kind; however, when the storm has passed the seed-centre of consciousness breathes 'I am divided for love's sake…' once more from the perfect stillness, revealing space beyond rational thinking, and a new creation.

The self uses the word 'my' to indicate its attributes and belongings, including the ideas with which the self clothes its own image. MY=36=MASK and MAN, whose sense of self is far more complicated than that of a woman. WOMAN=ME=ONE=46 is symbolic of unity, one-ness, a singularity with a negative charge rather than a positive charge. The isolation that comes with Womanhood is the opposite of the loneliness of Manhood. MY is generated by ME=46=WOMAN; MAN=SUN is designed to emit the spark of life and WOMAN=ABYSS is designed to receive it. Woman is the image of the Goddess divided for love's sake: WOMAN=ONE=46=I=23x2 or 11=HAD the manifestation of Nuit.

Woman

Womanhood never needs to be proved or tested. The adult human female is capable of creating another human life by virtue of the menstrual cycle. The ova in her body are present from birth and contain representations of the physiology of the previous generation whereas sperm cells contain a representation of the male physiology as it is at the time, being produced in the adult human male and stored in his body for up to ten weeks. This is why ancestry is traced through the female line, and why virginity is prized. The unbroken hymen indicates that sexual intercourse has not occurred, and therefore the sanctity of the womb has been maintained, the best guarantee for the paternity of future children. Losing virginity is a formidable rite of passage for a woman. It is possible that circumcision was devised to represent the same physical sacrifice. Be that as it may, these physical factors give a woman an organic understanding of sacrifice and the meaning of division for love's sake.

Woman is also inextricably linked with 93 since this is the value of both MOTHER and VIRGIN. Moreover, WOMAN=SORROW. She knows the sorrows of division and separation physically as well as emotionally, and she is subject to change from day to day. She gives birth to Life and brings Change into the world, causing and provoking sorrow. Woman is the initiator and teacher who sets the hero on his magical journey, which is not unlike the magical journey of a woman except that where his positive ego consciousness is negated to receive spiritual force, a woman's negativity is already receptive and she positively takes responsibility for the choice of force that she permits to dwell within her physical Temple.

TIME

Time/Nature/Virgin/Mother, 93, is between Heaven and Earth. 93 is the symbol of the division for love's sake and the uniting thereof, a pattern that resonates repeatedly throughout the English Qaballistic system. 93 represents the formula of Unity by Denial, or Division by Affirmation. It is the action of 93=TIME to give birth to the evolution of Nature.

Quantum physics has shown that for an event to materialise out of the multitude of probable events it must be observed, so it follows that Life must be present to observe the first Now moment of Time. Life, Now, and Time are therefore fundamental principles of reality, an interdependent trinity of primal concepts existing at the Creation of the Manifest Universe. This creation happens for love's sake according to *Liber Al*. Love is the creating force. Time and Now need Life as an expression of Love: Life and Time need Now as a focus for Love: Now and Life need Time as a matrix for Love. It is impossible to state which comes first. These are the factors that are involved in the manifestation that is Creation, according to English Qaballa.

LIFE=68=CHANGE. All that lives must change or is subject to change. This is the Law (6) expressed as Infinity (8).

TIME=93=MOTHER, from whom all Life is born.

NOW=24=GOD is also of course present at Creation.

TIME + NOW, 93+24=117, the value of THE LIGHT, (Manifest Kether) and BREATHED which joins up neatly with BREATH=86 the reward of Life/Change, emphasising the combined characteristics of God/Now and the Mother/Time. LIFE + GOD, 68+24=92=FEET the part of the body ruled by Pisces/Nothing; the feet in contact with the Earth provide for balance and for movement. LIFE + TIME, 68+93=161, where 6 is LAW balanced between 1 and 1, splitting 11 with the harmony that the number 6 always represents.

TIME+LIFE+NOW=185=REASON+ EMOTION, the extremes of Mind experience either side of the Middle Pillar. This gematria applies to the self-creating personal consciousness. As soon as there is consciousness of Life, self-aware in the Now, Time transfers the moment into the past. The consciousness of existence is continuously refreshed in the matrix of Time/Life/Now/.

TIME=93 ensures the evolution of ORIGINAL=93 phenomena. Magic is a negotiation with its inexorable flow.

LIFE=68=JESUS. English Qaballistic gematria enables a coherent reassessment of the symbol behind the name, removed from the establishment of church and state, independent of historical argument. JESUS=68=KRISHNA. Life itself is a deified force, characteristically child-like, generous, compassionate, and mirthful, whose divine responsibilities include answering sincere prayers and requests for aid, bestowing mercy and healing, and loving all unreservedly. The correspondence of Jesus with the Hindu love-god Krishna is uncomplicated. Sometimes regarded as the Supreme God, Krishna is a god of protection and intimate tenderness. This reinterpretation of Jesus removes the symbol from its problematic historic religious setting, placing it in the context of the English Qaballistic system, where Jesus gives love unconditionally as the positive embodiment of the Goddess. He is the Son of His Mother, enacting Her Will as the force known as LIFE=CHANGE. The Company of Heaven includes every deity and divine being known to humanity, all have Life and all are answerable to Jesus.

GOD

NOW has the same value as GOD, an English word with Germanic roots meaning 'the dweller in the grave-mound' which indicates the chthonic nature of the deity and its spiritual environment, the afterlife. It was the best choice for the Bible translators attempting to clarify the various Names and Titles attributed to the Deity in the Hebrew tradition. In EQ God is the source that is always happening, from the first created moment to this present moment and every moment revealed in between. Now/God is thus omnipresent. Moreover, God does not have human morality with which to judge and punish sinners; God simply exists, a primal force in and beyond the universe of human consciousness, the immanent ancestral spirit of all. These ideas, not taken from any particular theology, present an alternative understanding of the nature of God that is both free from religious doctrine and psychologically secure. Naturally GOD=DOG, the associations with the spirit-world being too obvious to require further description.

GOD=24=T, a simple cross; interestingly enough, in the common alphabet the 24th letter is another cruciform, the X, resembling a quarter-rotation of the lower-case letter t. Both x and + symbols are used also by mathematicians, supporting the association of the Deity with the science of numbers. X=DAY, a period of T=24 hours. Of course, CROSS adds to 42, which in E. Qaballistic terms is the reward of 24: in magical tradition the Cross is that of Matter, the symbol of the four Elements in equilibrium; the four Cardinal directions and the true Crossroads, as well as the more specific Calvary Cross and its variations. This affirms the relationship between God and the mechanisms of life in manifestation; and this is indicated again in that most magical substance BLOOD=42.

God in the EQ system is the unfolding essence of the Universe, always coming into being. The word may be taken as loosely describing the whole business of the Supernal Triad in the Hebrew system. GOD is the primary word-symbol of the ever-present liminal design of manifestation evidenced by observable natural laws. The gematria within the word supports this; GO indicates movement or motion, a fundamentally necessary characteristic of the manifest universe, confirmed by D=6=LAW. Therefore, God appears simply as inexorable force, with no fixed interactive attributes such as mercy or wrath, but eternally mobile and capable of instant modification. This definition bypasses the denominations of religion and atheism without provoking psychological conflicts of denial or delusion. God is a continuous state of becoming, allowing certainty to exist in the present which in turn promotes faith in the future. FAITH has the same value as SPACE in EQ; magically this is a space within Time where events may occur in accordance with the magician's Will.

GOD=WAND. This is the magical Weapon most associated with magical Will, Purpose, Intent, and Desire. The generative qualities of the Now moment are associated with the magical weapon of positive force which is usually seen as phallic, although this does not impute any gender to God in EQ since God is not delineated on a human scale as an entity, but described in human terms as a continuing event. The Wand is also the distinguishing sign of a messenger, being the means of carrying a message coded into knotted strings, seals, inscriptions, or other markings; the inside may even be hollowed out for greater protection and concealment of the message during its journey. The pressure of the unverbalised message is the Fiery part, it is a Word ready to be spoken, when it will become a creature of Air. In operations of sex magic therefore, great attention must be given to the preparation of the male ejaculate since its message is essentially a distillation of experience condensed by ambition.

The continual manifestation of the trinitarian Time/Life/Now is completed with a fourth principle of location in space, 'here'. HERE=66=HEART and EARTH, indicating both the physical and the spiritual reality. 66 is a multiple of 11 and symbolises the Law expressed as the Law: all the double digits are their own reward. Adding the location to the idea of CREATION=119 gives the sum 119 + 66 = 185=TIME/LIFE/NOW, which shows that positioned creation correlates with the Now moment in Time as observed by Life. The development of three into four is in the natural evolution of the point to the line, the plane, and the solid. These are the conditions under which Manifestation occurs. 4=H, the sound of an out-breath and the first letter of *Liber Al*.

The Four Archetypes

In EQ the FIRST=82 corresponds with the FOURTH=82, suggesting four component parts manifesting as ONE=46, which is 4 expressed as LAW=6. The LUNAR=46 cycle is FOURFOLD=87=MONTHLY. The four phases measure the interval of the lunar month, upon which the conventional calendar months are based. The quarters between the full moon and the dark moon are marked by the two gibbous moons. The new moon crescent is the first quarter and follows the darkened old moon of the last quarter. In the third quarter the full moon begins to wane, and in the second quarter the moon's light increases.

These four distinct archetypal characteristics provide the means to reassess the qualities associated with the four Elements of western tradition, Earth, Air, Fire, Water, with their magical weapons and cardinal points.

The North is the place of darkness, the midnight position in an astrological chart, and thus appropriate to the dark phase of the Moon and the Crone. Earth is the Element, by association with funerary mysteries of regeneration and metamorphosis. CRONE=71=VENUS which accounts for the legends of transformation of the old woman into the beautiful maiden.

The purity ascribed to Air is easily correlated with the virginal crescent of the Moon's first quarter, and the Eastern horizon. Neither is the Sword inimical, for virgin goddesses are often armed and dangerous.

The Cup is attributable to the Mother, and the third quarter of the lunar cycle in which star-lit night is born as moonlight decreases. In the West the Mother balances the Virgin. Both MOTHER and VIRGIN add to 93.

The South is the astrological midday and the place of greatest power, appropriate to the waxing Moon. The magical weapon of the Enchantress is the Wand: she has her own power and fire of devotion, and it is her magic that conjures sparks of life from the mutilated body of the dead God himself. The mythologies of Isis and Persephone overlap and join in the Underworld. This goddess is independent and unrestricted, self-reliant, and responsible, and very wise. ENCHANTRESS=142, the first numeric value counting from 1 in the vocabulary of *Liber Al* to have no single word attribution, giving the numeric symbol a distinctly abstract characteristic. MOON+SCORPIO=142.

The archetypal roles are interchangeable to some extent, the significant point being that there are four rather than three. The balancing of the elements within the psyche is proper for any magical operation. Coherent linkages between the external objectively observable realities and the magician's internal conscious domain create an interface of certainties based upon experience, so that instead of studying a given system of correspondences from the outside one finds oneself at the centre of the sphere, and the interconnectedness of everything becomes apparent. The quietus may only last a moment, but the knowledge of it is permanent.

The Scarlet Woman

The idea of a fourth lunar goddess provides a general context in which to examine *Liber Al*'s SCARLET WOMAN = 128. The renaissance of this goddess is a feature of the general revolution in consciousness that has been slowly dawning upon humanity since the discovery of Pluto in 1930. The name APHRODITE adds to 128 by EQ, indicating that the primary powers of the Scarlet Woman are Beauty and Love, making her dangerously desirable. Pity and compassion and tenderness do not visit her heart but reside there permanently. Her love is unconditional, her virtue is unassailable. She is easy to worship but difficult to know.

The number 128 represents the Woman (=1) of the WORD=28. The number 28 correlates with the average number of days in the lunar cycle and with the number of characters in II:76; it is the value of ANKH, the well-known Egyptian symbol of Life. The reward of the Word is 82=SCARLET. 82 is also the value of BALANCED, FIRST, and FOURTH, indicating that her gift is the harmonised quaternary structure of 44 (4x11) = LOVE. The number 82 represents the completion of personal psychological architecture pertaining to the status of 128.

SCARLET WOMAN=128=BAPHOMET.

The Scarlet Woman correlates with Baphomet: she has equilibrated the Elements in her psyche and has the knowledge of what she is Not, and of what she Is, balanced within her consciousness. She is the Master of her own temple wherein she speaks her Word. In *Liber Al* she is also called the SCARLET CONCUBINE where CONCUBINE=146=SAGITTARIUS, the alchemical rectification of Man and Beast. 28=HOLY and WORD is repeated in the value of SCARLET CONCUBINE=228, which is the value of PRINCE-PRIEST. These titles refer to attained conscious conditions, and it is necessary to recognise that the condition itself is impermanent since one cannot remain in the ecstasy of vision as Time continues to bring Change; however, the effect of the experience may last longer than one lifetime. The numbers 128 and 228 both express Infinity in the final digit, 8. The number 12 represents the encircling Zodiac, and 22 represents the justified sacrifice associated with the Prince-priest.

The Scarlet Woman is named BABALON=65. This is a true name of the GODDESS=65. WATER also adds to 65, and as that Element is symbolic of the female archetype so this is a simple but effective demonstration of EQ. This also explains how She can be defiled and yet remain pure.

The primary goddess in the *Book of the Law* is Nuit, the Queen of space and stars. NUIT=FIRE, and BABALON=WATER, and SOPHIA=EARTH; these Elements are attributable to the Goddess, and AIR=MAN/SUN is the complementary Element in this cosmology.

65 is the value of HONEY and of WINE, emphasising the sweet inebriation offered by Babalon, while Nuit is UNKNOWN (=78) and TRUE (=78). The number 78 represents O expressed as Infinity, and the division for love's sake described in *Liber Al* as 'None…and Two' that in EQ is the Creation. 65 is Law expressed as Energy. 65 = DREAM and EYE, GNOSIS and WISDOM, indicating the conscious experiences and effect of Babalon that may confer the qualifications of a SIBYL=65. The reward of Babalon is 56=CUP, which is as neat and tidy a correspondence as any. Babalon in EQ represents the finest qualities of unconditional Love, symbolised by the Cup. This is not to say that Babalon loves indiscriminately, for WISDOM=65 and 56=WISE. She is the Keeper of the Cauldron of Life and the Bearer of the GRAIL=49=MOON, the Woman Clothed With The Sun.

EPILOGUE

English Qaballa modifies the thinking/speaking mind by usage, enabling the magician to think symbolically and develop conscious structures other than arguments of reason and logic. The usefulness of applying numbers to letters is straightforward enough: the numeric value of a word becomes a factor linking other words of the same value, whose literal and symbolic meanings may then elucidate and clarify each other, leading to a better understanding of the ideas involved. English Qaballistic correspondences join the dots from the limitless void of infinite space to the material substance of human life, making an organically harmonious framework for magical consciousness. The Mystery is what it is; gematria makes a bridge between the symbolic language of words and the symbolic language of numbers which more closely resemble the inexpressible interconnected harmony of the manifest Universe. It is the pressure of necessity, the energy of Formation, that makes magic work.

The in-text correspondences resulting from the application of EQ to the *Book of the Law* indicates a comprehensive magical system that harmonises with other systems instead of conflicting with them, which is important for psychological health. English

Qaballa is not restricted by its source, for study of the gematria must sooner or later include the same significant English words and their values. Everyone will eventually notice that 'cross' has the same value as 'star.' The conceptualisation of correspondence between CROSS and STAR will be subjective, but there can be no doubt that there is an objective numerical connection between the two word-symbols.

One of the most rewarding uses of magic is the discovery and integration of spiritual consciousness and that part of the psyche that is always watching, sometimes leading and sometimes compelling; the doubt and fear of its apparent existence matched only by the doubt and fear of there being in fact no such thing, this being the layer between the personal individual waking mind and its source. This is more or less a quest for an objective truth that resonates equally both within the individual and in the infinitely wider reality of the everlasting universe, some meaningful relationship between the inner self and the outer environment, a self-knowledge with contextual regard to the general progress of everything else. It is the prerogative of magic to heal the spiritual divisions inherent to the human condition of mortality.

James Lees, who discovered the Key and coined the name "English Qaballa," recognised the possibility of uncovering a new system in the numeric correspondences of *Liber Al*, since they extend into every system expressed in the English language, enabling comparative analysis of religious and spiritual wisdom of all the ages from an alternative E. Qaballistic point of view. Lees was primarily interested in the psychological benefits of EQ and the potential for ritual undertakings to mitigate and prepare for the worst astrological influences that the Fates inflict upon an individual. In theory, the correspondences of EQ should provide a metaphysical framework capable of extending consciousness beyond the thinking/speaking mind to the unattached stillness attainable by following other established spiritual practices, without the necessary adherence to religious regimes. This is the 'consciousness of the continuity of existence' mentioned in *Liber Al*. Ultimately, EQ should improve life by making preparations for death with some conscious linkage to the immortal soul. This is one of the unstated aims of magic and one of the functions of religion, most often accomplished by means of ritualised cycles corresponding with observations of natural phenomena, and by deliberately maintaining awareness of the spiritual presence of the deceased. In the ancient world it was a foundational sacred purpose. The numbers generated by EQ suggested the ritualising of certain astrological phenomena to achieve these results. These theories took many years to prove before practical ritual experiments involving the full Libra-Scorpio-Sagittarius-Capricorn sequence were carried out.

The balancing of the reasoning intellect with the emotional intellect is one of the foremost challenges in magic; success is facilitated by the Sun-Venus ritual indicated by EQ, the celestial alchemical refinement of the pentagram producing an integration of the Elements in the consciousness of the operator. This transformation is known as the Ordeal X, and upon completion the candidate will be of what *Liber Al* refers to as the Lover Grade, with the elements of the psyche balanced in the manifest personality and contact established with the consciousness of universal Love which is often called 'Christ consciousness'.

The initiations resulting from E. Qaballistic stellar magic are similar to those spiritual experiences that magicians inevitably encounter when the attention of the Universe at large is alerted to their presence. The alterations in consciousness are such as have been described by mystics everywhere; naturally, since the Mystery remains the same for all Eternity, and it is only the interpretations, and the names, that change. EQ contains the same Beauty and Truth that is the core of all spirituality, concealed and revealed in the patterns of its gematria.

Appendix 1

While I was writing this book two ceremonial magicians completed the sequence of 418 rituals with results that closely paralleled or coincided with the records of the first experiment, including the feeling that there was still some work to do in the way of finalising the process. At the end of the original 418 experiment Jim and I had written additional rituals to mark the Sun-Moon conjunction in Capricorn and the ingress of the Sun into Aquarius and Pisces, and when the question arose again independently it came as a proof of the system. These three rituals are included here.

OBSERVATION OF NEW MOON IN CAPRICORN

To be performed at midday with the Sun and Moon applying to conjunct in Capricorn.

At or on the Altar, the Sword, incense, and a single large candle inscribed with the symbol 2112.

Face South, stand with your feet apart, arms upraised and curving forwards (Sign of Isis in Welcome), and say

By the Power of the Victory of the Light of Heaven, I Am!

I am come with the Moon to the place of the Phoenix. I am the Master in Thy Temple, by my Truth, my Will and my Love. Blessed be Thy Fire!

Light candle

I offer this incense in sacrifice to the Company of Heaven! - blessed be thou, creature of Earth and Fire: be thou a grateful perfume that is acceptable to the Time.

Light incense (Frankincense)

I invoke the Joy of the Living Truth in the House of the Blessed Goat! The Begetter and the Manifester unto the Light and of the Light! The Grace of the Worlds!

Contemplate the candle flame as your own spark of existence for a moment. Then snuff out the flame with the right hand and with the same fingers make an equal-armed cross over the breastbone, saying

I transfer the Eternal Light to my heart.

Within me is the Flame of every Star! The Shower of the Life of Earth! Strong, and the Immortal Fire! Life in the Eternal Now of Time! There is no god that is not part of me.

Take the Sword and make the Sign of the invoking Earth Pentagram. Replace the Sword and say

I go forth with the light of Heaven and by the Power of Love to do my Will upon the Earth.

So mote it be.

Amen.

SUN-AQUARIUS

To be performed in the hour of dawn when the Sun is between 0 and 3 degrees of Aquarius. At or on the Altar, the Sword, the Pantacle of Ash, and a single large candle.

Face East.

This is the Time of Awakening, when the Sun is in the House of The Light-Bearer. I open this Temple of the Stars to wake the Keeper of the Vessel of Eternal Life and the Sword of Truth.

Light incense (cedar)

Blessed be Thou, creature of Earth and Fire, may Thy perfume sanctify my way.

I awake! I am he/she who has borne the ordeals of Love and walked the Lunar Path with faith under the night-stars. I have been given the Word that is between Heaven and Earth.

In the Name of the Master of Life, Whose Numbers and Words are 4, 6, 3, 8, A, B, K, 2, 4, A:

Make the sign of a Calvary Cross.

For the Honour of the Mother Virgin Who unites and divides Heaven and Earth, Whose Numbers and Words are L, G, M, O, R, 3, Y, X:

Make the sign of an X Cross over the Calvary Cross

In the Presence of the Eternal Now, Whose Numbers and Words are 24, 89, R, P, S, T, O, V, A, L:

Make the sign of an Equal-armed Cross over the X and the Calvary Crosses.

Here:

Make a circle around the three Crosses.

It is my Will to partake of the Living Light as the Sun awakened from winter sleep. I invoke Thee by the Star and by the Blood and by the Kiss.

Kiss the candle and light it, and say

As the light flows from the vessel of the stars and returns to the Earth so may this light be an emblem of the Truth.

Contemplate the candle flame as your own spark of existence for a moment. Then snuff out the flame with the right hand and with the same fingers make an equal-armed cross over the breastbone, saying

The light of the Sun is reborn upon the Earth and burns in my heart.

Take up the Sword with the right hand and hold it vertically at chest level, hilt upwards.

I serve the Truth.

Turn to the South holding the Sword, and say

My Wand was broken that my Will be Thy Will.

Turn to the West holding the Sword, and say

I serve Love.

Turn to the North holding the Sword, and say

I am steadfast.

Turn to the East holding the Sword. Kiss the cross of the hilt, then put the point over the centre of the Pantacle and say

I am the self-slain servant of Heaven, Master of the Temple, Lord of the Spirits of the Stars. I invoke SADALMELIK, SADALSUUD, SADACHIBA, ALBALI. Hear me! and bring thy blessing unto me and serve me in the Ineffable Eternal Light.

Put the Sword down. With the right hand transfer the living light in the breast to the Pantacle by tracing an equal-armed cross over it. Say

The Stars are my earthly abode, in Life, Time, and Now, by Nuit the infinitely large and Hadit the infinitely small and all that is between them.
So mote it be.
Amen.

Give the Sign of Silence.

SUN-PISCES

To be performed in the hour before dawn when the Sun is in the second decanate of Pisces.

At or on the Altar, the Sword, the Pantacle of Ash, and a single candle which can be left safely to burn out.

Face East.

This is the Time of Dreaming, when the Sun is in the Sign of the Fishes. I open this Temple of the Stars to wake the Keeper of the Doorway Between Worlds.

Light incense (ambergris)

I sacrifice this perfume to the Company of Heaven.
In the Name of the Master of Life, Whose Numbers and Words are 4, 6, 3, 8, A, B, K, 2, 4, A:

Make the sign of a Calvary Cross.

For the Honour of the Mother Virgin Who unites and divides Heaven and Earth, Whose Numbers and Words are L, G, M, O, R, 3, Y, X:

Make the sign of an X Cross over the Calvary Cross

In the Presence of the Eternal Now, Whose Numbers and Words are 24, 89, R, P, S, T, O, V, A, L:

Make the sign of an Equal-armed Cross over the X and the Calvary Crosses.

Here:

Make a circle around the three Crosses. Take up the Sword with the left hand and hold it vertically at chest level, hilt upwards.

I am he/she Thy Chosen, who has borne the ordeals of Love, walked the Lunar Path with faith under the night-stars and come to this threshold of the future. It is my Will to invoke the Keeper of the Gates, Ra Hoor Khut, the Reward of the Word, that my Sword may serve the Truth and my Pantacle may become a new Earth.

Replace the Sword.

I invoke thee, Ra Hoor Khut, Thou who art Nothing in all things, from whom I invoke my spirits and arm myself for the Rebirth to come. I stand on the threshold of a new life. I invoke the Great Stars AL RISCHA and ALPHERG, to bear witness – there is no grace, there is no guilt. I seek nothing for myself. I ask for the blessing of the Company of Heaven upon all* who are dear to my heart, that the spirits of the Firmament bring the flame of Joy into their hearts.

Light candle.

May they be blessed by the Living Glory of the Stars!
The flame that burns in my heart is renewed in the moment to be.

Contemplate the candle flame as your own spark of existence for a moment, then say

The ending of the words is the Word (silently) *ABRAHADABRA.*
Amen.

*These may be living or dead; speak their names as appropriate.

Appendix 2

This is an all-purpose invocatory prayer composed according to the principles that have been presented heretofore.

Blessed be the Name of the Lord whose number is 68, for Thou art Life and the Giver of Life, Thou art Change and the Lord of Change. Thy nature is the Love of God, and the Love of God is God. Thou healeth me when I am sick, Thou lifteth me up when I am fallen, Thou makest my Way clear when all is dark. My life is Thy life, and Thy Life is my Life, for Thou art the Life in all things. Thy Symbol is the Cross of Life, which I wear in my breast, and in my mind, for Thou art the Brilliance that is the Continuity of Existence. Amen.

Appendix 3

This is an all-purpose blessing composed according to the same principles as mentioned above.

In the Name of the Lord of Life, for the Honour of the Mother, in the presence of the Eternal Now, Here! (Clap hands, stamp foot, beat chest, ring bell, or make other positive noisy gesture.)

INDEX

Fire 10, 40
Water 25, 40

G

H

I

J

K

L

M

in Scorpio 14

N

Neptune 1, 25
New Aeon 3, 9
Nuit 10, 11, 12, 30, 45

O

Old Aeon 3
Ordeal X 20, 21, 49
O.T.O. 2

P

Perfected Tree 23-24
Persephone 41
Pisces 1, 23, 25, 26, 34
Pluto 43

R

Ra Hoor Khut 23
Rex Mundi 20

S

Sagittarius 20, 48
Scarlet Woman 21, 43, 44
Scorpio 12, 13, 14, 15, 17, 20, 23, 25, 28, 41
Stele of Revealing 10
Sun 18, 20, 21, 30, 45, 49
Sun-Venus 21, 49
Supernal Triad 37

T

*9 7 8 1 9 1 5 9 3 3 2 1 8 *